About the Book

Cause and Effect for grades 5–6 has been designed to ▢ students to practice cause and effect skills. The book bring▢ students the application of cause and effect skills through ▢ areas they study every day. Additionally, character skills are ▢▢▢▢▢ed as students work through practical life applications to examine consequences of actions through critical thinking. Students of a wide range of abilities will find this book valuable. Activities are written to guide students carefully, yet challenge them to move forward based on personal ability.

• •

Table of Contents

You Pick

Each picture shows an effect. Circle the answer that tells the correct cause.

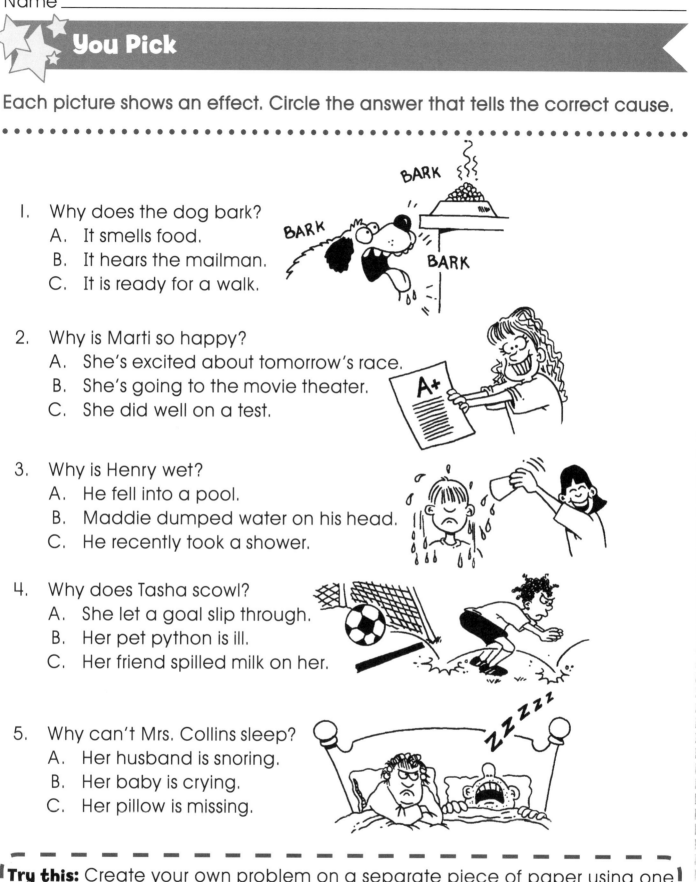

1. Why does the dog bark?
   A. It smells food.
   B. It hears the mailman.
   C. It is ready for a walk.

2. Why is Marti so happy?
   A. She's excited about tomorrow's race.
   B. She's going to the movie theater.
   C. She did well on a test.

3. Why is Henry wet?
   A. He fell into a pool.
   B. Maddie dumped water on his head.
   C. He recently took a shower.

4. Why does Tasha scowl?
   A. She let a goal slip through.
   B. Her pet python is ill.
   C. Her friend spilled milk on her.

5. Why can't Mrs. Collins sleep?
   A. Her husband is snoring.
   B. Her baby is crying.
   C. Her pillow is missing.

Try this: Create your own problem on a separate piece of paper using one of these questions: Why does Goldilocks run away? Why is José in trouble?

Spotlight on Reading

Cause and Effect
Grades 5–6

Frank Schaffer

An imprint of Carson-Dellosa Publishing LLC
Greensboro, North Carolina

Credits

Layout and Cover Design: Van Harris

Development House: The Research Masters

Cover Photo: Image Copyright gsmad, 2011 Used under license from Shutterstock.com

 This book has been correlated to state, common core state, national, and Canadian provincial standards. Visit *www.carsondellosa.com* to search for and view its correlations to your standards.

Frank Schaffer

An imprint of Carson-Dellosa Publishing LLC

PO Box 35665

Greensboro, NC 27425 USA

www.carsondellosa.com

ISBN 978-16-099-6485-6

03-147137784

Emilio

Read each pair of sentences. Write **C** on the line by the cause. Write **E** on the line by the effect.

1. Emilio's family moved. _____
   Emilio missed his friends Carlos and John. _____

2. Emilio's sister was happy. _____
   She had the kitten she always wanted. _____

3. Emilio's mother was taking classes at the college. _____
   She was learning new things. _____

4. Emilio's father got a job at the TV station. _____
   He met celebrities. _____

5. Emilio decided to walk down to the creek. _____
   He wanted to see the tadpoles. _____

6. There was a drought. _____
   There was not much water in the creek. _____

7. The water was evaporating fast. _____
   The tadpoles would not have time to grow into frogs. _____

8. Emilio ran to the house to get a plastic jar. _____
   He wanted to save the tadpoles. _____

> **Try this:** Read the cause. Write a possible effect.
> **Cause:** Emilio gave some of the tadpoles a safe place to live.

Name _____

Read each sentence. Write the cause and effect in the appropriate blanks.

• •

1. Andre earned money by mowing lawns for his neighbors.
   Cause:_____

   Effect: _____

2. Andre saved his earnings until he could afford to buy a new bike.
   Cause:_____

   Effect: _____

3. Becca forgot to water the plant on her windowsill, and the plant wilted.
   Cause:_____

   Effect: _____

4. The plant became healthy when Becca watered it.
   Cause:_____

   Effect: _____

5. Having studied very hard, Carla finished the test easily.
   Cause:_____

   Effect: _____

6. Carla made a perfect score on the test, which brought her grade to an A.
   Cause:_____

   Effect: _____

Name_____

The Lion and the Mouse

Read the following version of Aesop's fable. Match each cause to the correct effect. Write the letter of the effect on the line by the cause.

• •

A lion was sleeping peacefully when he felt something scurry across his giant, velvety paws. He opened his large, amber eyes to see a little mouse, standing on its hind legs, staring back at him. The small creature appeared to be frozen with terror.

"How dare you wake me from my slumber?" roared the lion. "Tonight, I shall dine upon fresh mouse, so at least I might have a snack for this inconvenience."

The mouse shivered and cried out, "Please forgive me, King Lion. Spare my life. One day, I may have the opportunity to repay your great kindness by saving your life."

The lion looked at the tiny mouse and felt the corners of his mouth twitch. The very idea of the miniscule rodent saving his life was the most hilarious thing he had ever heard. His mouth opened, and the mouse prepared for the end, but instead of being eaten, the lion let loose a deep rich, laugh. Tears of laughter ran down his regal face. "Go, Sir Mouse. You are too entertaining to eat."

Seasons passed, and one day, while the mouse was scavenging for food, he came upon a horrible sight. The lion was bound head to tail by thick, strong ropes. Exhausted from fighting his bonds, the lion lay motionless—helpless and defeated. The mouse scurried up to the lion's nose and said, "I am here to repay my debt." He chewed and gnawed at the ropes that bound the lion until the great beast was free. The lion stood, stretched, and shook his glorious mane. He lowered his noble head in respect to the mouse and said, "Your debt has been paid, and I thank you."

Causes	**Effects**
_____ 1. The mouse walked on the lion's paws.	A. The lion was free.
_____ 2. The mouse pleaded for his life.	B. The lion awoke.
_____ 3. The mouse chewed through the ropes.	C. The lion could not escape.
_____ 4. Hunters tied the lion with rope.	D. The lion let the mouse live.

The Right Cause

Look at the causes by the pictures. Read the effects in each effect bank. Match three effects to each cause. Write the letter of each answer in the balloons.

· ·

Effect Bank

A. has never been beaten in wrestling

B. punches holes in titanium with his fist

C. volunteers to baby-sit for free

D. can pick up Neanderthal Nate

E. helps me with homework

F. does extra chores to help around the house

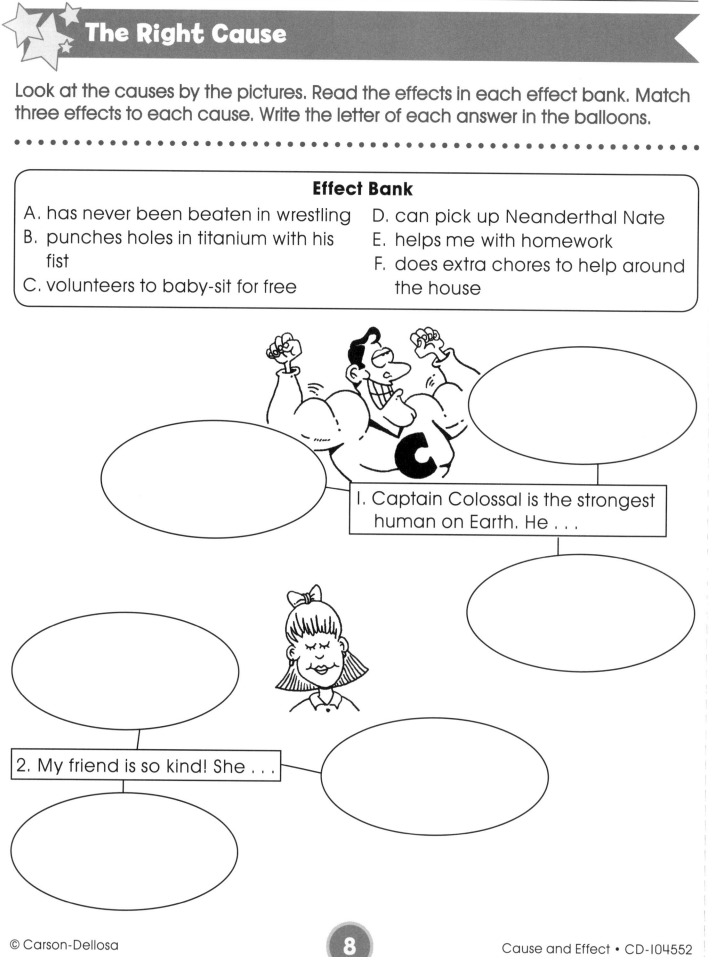

1. Captain Colossal is the strongest human on Earth. He . . .

2. My friend is so kind! She . . .

The Right Cause (cont.)

Effect Bank

G. grabbed flashlights and blankets
H. looks up at the sky every night
I. hid under his bed

J. dashed to our cellar
K. called everyone together
L. went to tell his parents

3. Ben is sure he saw a UFO. He . . .

4. The storm was heading straight for our town. We . . .

9

Name _____

Instantly Hot and Cold

Read the passage and answer the questions.

• •

Have you ever been injured and used an instant hot or cold pack? Instant hot and cold packs use a chemical reaction to help you with your sprained ankle or sore back.

A chemical reaction occurs when two chemical substances mix and form different substances. Sometimes a chemical reaction releases heat. When a chemical called calcium chloride is mixed with water, the reaction releases heat and makes the container feel warm.

Sometimes a chemical reaction absorbs heat from the environment. When a chemical called ammonium nitrate is mixed with water, the reaction absorbs heat. The container feels cold.

Instant hot and cold packs are plastic pouches filled with a dry chemical—usually calcium chloride or ammonium nitrate. Inside the pouch is another pouch filled with water. When the hot or cold pack is squeezed, the inner pouch breaks. Shaking the instant pack helps the water mix completely with the chemical. A chemical reaction occurs, and the instant pack becomes either hot or cold.

1. You might need a hot or cold pack because _____

    _____ .

2. You might use a pack with calcium chloride because _____

    _____ .

3. You might use a pack with ammonium nitrate because _____

    _____ .

4. You must squeeze the hot or cold pack to _____

    _____ .

5. You must shake a hot or cold pack to _____

    _____ .

         Cause and Effect • CD-104552

Boy Meets Reality

Look at the six effects below. Match each effect to the correct set of causes below. Write the answers on the lines.

Effects

He took too long in the bathroom.	He went shopping.
He was late to school.	He went to the beach.
He saw a movie.	He got an A+ on the assignment.

1. The humidity was unbearable.
    The summer sun shone fiercely.
    Abel was free to relax.
    Effect: _____

2. Cody had no good clothes.
    He needed school supplies.
    He hoped to see friends at the mall.
    Effect: _____

3. Everyone was talking about it.
    Dani offered to take him.
    Emmett just received his allowance.
    Effect: _____

4. Pablo could not find his books.
    He overslept again.
    He took a long time eating breakfast.
    Effect: _____

5. Owen showered for forty minutes.
    He played with his hair for ten minutes.
    He stood before the mirror for twenty minutes.
    Effect: _____

6. Lamar went to the media lab.
    He organized his notes.
    He followed the instructions.
    Effect: _____

11

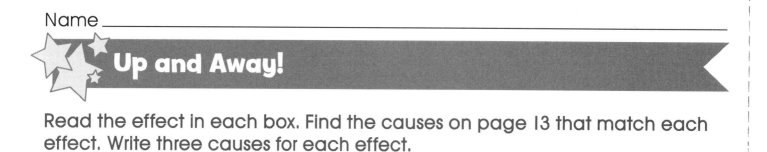

Up and Away!

Read the effect in each box. Find the causes on page 13 that match each effect. Write three causes for each effect.

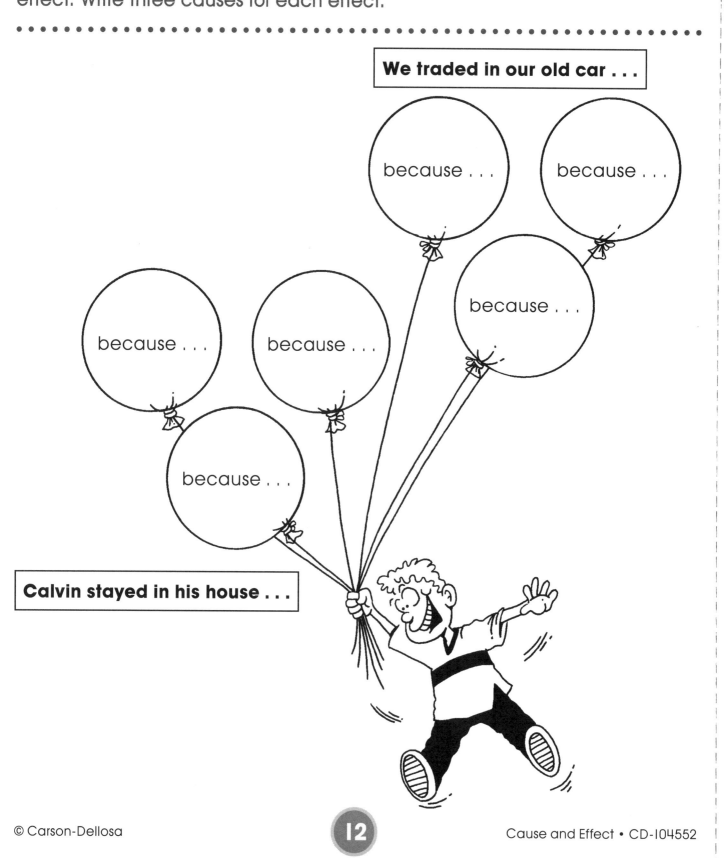

We traded in our old car . . .

because . . .

because . . .

because . . .

because . . .

because . . .

because . . .

Calvin stayed in his house . . .

Cause and Effect • CD-104552

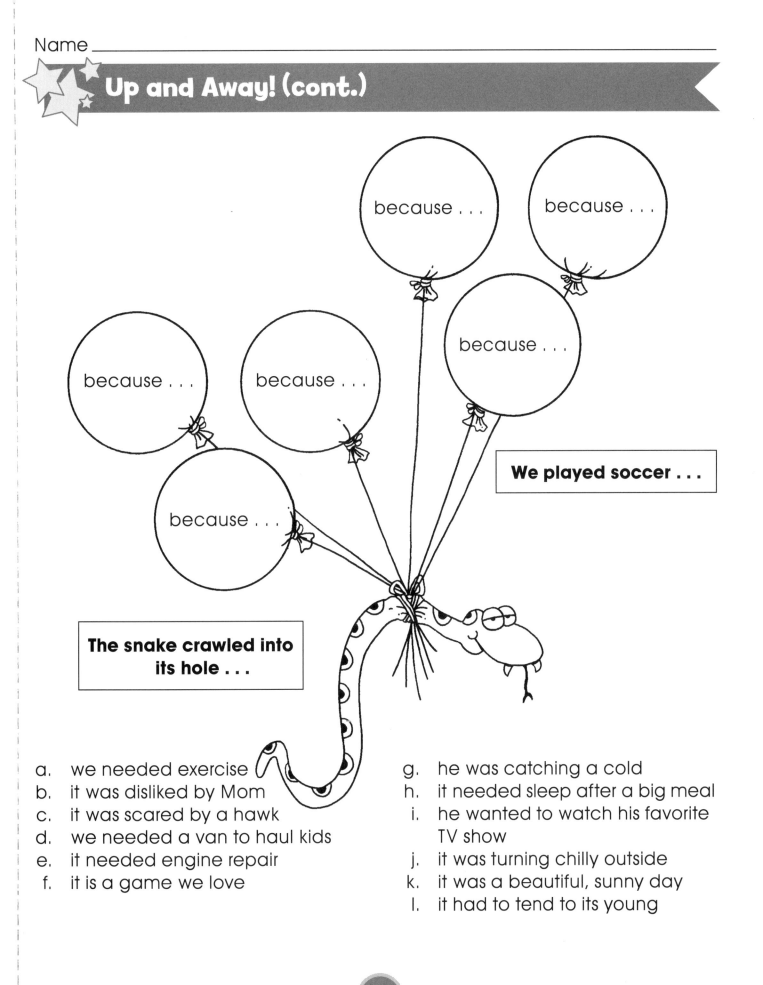

because . . .

because . . .

because . . .

because . . .

because . . .

because . . .

We played soccer . . .

The snake crawled into its hole . . .

a. we needed exercise
b. it was disliked by Mom
c. it was scared by a hawk
d. we needed a van to haul kids
e. it needed engine repair
f. it is a game we love

g. he was catching a cold
h. it needed sleep after a big meal
i. he wanted to watch his favorite TV show
j. it was turning chilly outside
k. it was a beautiful, sunny day
l. it had to tend to its young

13

Name _____

Sweeter Than Honey

Scientists make **conclusions** from their observations. The conclusion is the effect. Read the numbered set of observations (causes). Match a conclusion to each set. Write the answers on the lines.

• •

Conclusions

Bee colonies are complex.

Farmers depend on bees.

Flowering plants are vital to bees.

Bees are diverse insects.

1. Pollen is a protein source.
   Pollen is also a food source for bee larvae.
   Flower nectar is an energy source.
   Conclusion: _____

2. Bees are found in most world regions.
   Bees may be yellow, black, gray, blue, red, or green.
   Bees may range from 2 mm to 4 cm in length.
   Conclusion: _____

3. Semi-social bees live in colonies of two to seven.
   Each group consists of a queen and her daughter workers.
   Such colonies are temporary and can change.
   Conclusion: _____

4. Some bees produce honey.
   Beeswax is harvested from honeycombs to sell.
   Bees provide pollination required for many fruits and vegetables.
   Conclusion: _____

  Cause and Effect • CD-104552

Name _____

Underline the cause and circle the effect in each sentence.

• •

1. When Omar stubbed his toe, he cried out, "Ouch!"

2. The rain was coming into the house, so we shut the windows.

3. Because I was full from the tasty chicken soup, I slept like a baby.

4. Karen was disappointed when she missed an easy lay-up.

5. We made a model volcano for a science fair. It erupted when we mixed vinegar and baking soda.

6. At the airport, David could not sit still because he was excited to fly for the first time.

7. When the theater lights were turned on, I was blinded for a moment.

8. Because he is interested in modern art, Ted begged to see the newest art exhibit.

9. Tanya said, "Go fish!" because she had no kings.

⭐ Caption Capers

Match the causes with the effects. Write the letters of the answers on the lines under the pictures.

• •

Causes	**Effects**

Effects

A. Tomás went to Mrs. Kater's front door to apologize.

B. The fruit drink was nasty.

C. Betsy was tired the next day.

D. Derek ran away.

1.

_____

2.

_____

3.

_____

4.

_____

16

More Caption Capers

Match the causes with the effects. Write the letters of the answers on the lines under the pictures.

Effects	**Causes**

Effects

Causes

1.

_____

A. Because Bart's wife takes long showers . . .

B. Because Marianne hit a home run . . .

C. Because a storm was coming . . .

D. Because the car ran out of gas . . .

2.

_____

3.

_____

4.

_____

Traveling with the Corps

Underline the cause and circle the effect in each sentence.

. . . .

1. Because President Jefferson was interested in finding a water route for trade to the Pacific Ocean, he commissioned an expedition called the Corps of Discovery.

2. Sacagawea joined the Corps of Discovery when her husband Toussaint Charbonneau was hired as a guide.

3. Because she was Shoshone, Sacagawea could help Lewis and Clark's expeditionary force obtain food and supplies from her people.

4. As they began, Sacagawea carried her son on her back because he was only a baby.

5. To move the expedition's freight up river, the group hired a large keelboat.

6. Because of her herbal knowledge, Sacagawea's tasks included gathering edible plants for the Corps.

7. The young woman was surprised when she met her older brother, now a chief among her people.

8. Because her husband was officially hired by the expedition and she was not, Sacagawea received no personal compensation for her work.

9. There are conflicting reports about Sacagawea's later life, so historians consider her a puzzle.

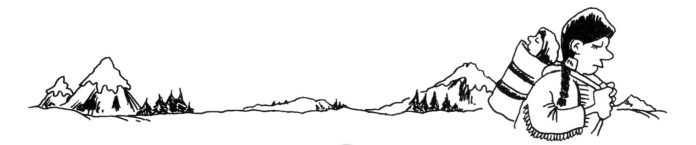

Picking the Cause

Read each pair of sentences. Circle the cause.

· ·

1. Madison and Ryan were late.
   The bus had a flat tire.

2. Josh needed help.
   He e-mailed Dylan.

3. Josh could not find his watch.
   It had slipped under his dresser.

4. Josh looked everywhere in his room.
   He hoped to find his grandfather's watch.

5. Dylan led the way to the house.
   He had the address.

6. The members of the Mystery Society were excited.
   It was their first case in a long time.

7. Ryan and Madison ran.
   They were late.

8. The house had a messy yard.
   It needed a lot of work.

9. The dresser was in Josh's room.
   Josh took the Mystery Society upstairs.

19

⭐ What Caused It?

Read each effect statement. Write two possible causes for each effect.

• •

1. Trisha's lunch box was empty.

    _____

    _____

2. Sadaf had no homework to do this weekend.

    _____

    _____

3. Caleb felt nauseous.

    _____

    _____

4. The chocolate-colored dog was wet.

    _____

    _____

5. The cornbread burned.

    _____

    _____

6. The coyote howled.

    _____

    _____

Try this: Write a story based on one of the above causes and effects.

What Happened?

Look at the six sets of causes below. Write the effect you might expect from each.

• •

1. The child stretched the balloon.
    He put it to his lips.
    He pursed his lips around the balloon's neck.
    Effect: _____

2. She was in such a hurry riding her bike.
    She carried her viola across the bars.
    She failed to see the rock on the street in front of her.
    Effect: _____

3. We had a tremendous snowstorm during the night.
    Winds gusted to 45 mph (72 km/h).
    The roads are blocked.
    Effect: _____

4. I ran as fast as I could.
    I passed all the other runners.
    I was not even tired.
    Effect: _____

5. I awoke and had my breakfast.
    I pulled out my toothbrush.
    I smeared toothpaste over the bristles.
    Effect: _____

6. Dani held her burger in her hand, even though she had
    already eaten a large lunch.
    Her pup looked up at her with those begging eyes.
    Sighing, the dog rested its head on her lap.
    Effect: _____

21

Chicken Coop

Read the story. Answer the questions on the next page.

• •

Sometimes my sister Teralynn gets excited. One morning Teralynn poked her head into my room to tell me, "Things are going crazy outside!" I didn't know what to think. I ignored her and stayed in my room to finish my math homework.

"Danny! You'd better get out here or Dad will be unhappy with you!" Teralynn said.

I jumped out of my seat then. I didn't want Dad unhappy. My brothers and sisters were outside, so I stepped off the porch and let the screen door slam behind me. I heard voices over by the barn, so I followed the screams and clucks. The chickens had escaped from their coop!

I dashed to the barn. All the way, I could hear beating wings and rooster crows and kids yelling. It was so bad, I couldn't tell the kids' sounds from the chickens'. I never even made it to the barn. Those chickens ran all over the yard. Davey and Missy chased after them, but they were not fast enough to catch a loose hen. Teralynn tried to restore order, telling the kids to catch the chickens.

We tried to push them back in through the barn door. No matter how we tried it, the chickens would not go into the barn.

"Teralynn," I said, "you fix the gate so they can't escape again. Missy and Davey, you grab those poles by the shed, and stand back out of the way by the fence. If those chickens come your way, make them go back."

I decided to let out Bonnie Belle. Bonnie is a big, shiny, black mare. She does not like chickens, and they do not trust her. Bonnie Belle is fast and tricky.

I let Bonnie out of the barn, and she saw those fluffy feathers. She flared her nostrils, picked up her ears, let out a whinny, and started galloping in wild circles around the yard.

The chickens clucked louder than ever. They scurried back to the barn and into their coop. It did not take more than three minutes. Missy and Teralynn shut the pen up, and that was that.

I took Bonnie by her harness. "That's it, girl. You did a good job," I said, and I fed her two cubes of sugar.

Chicken Coop (cont.)

Complete the following sentences.

1. Teralynn called to Danny because . . .

   _____

   _____

2. The speaker headed out the door because Teralynn . . .

   _____

   _____

3. The speaker headed toward the barn because . . .

   _____

   _____

4. When he heard clucks, the speaker knew . . .

   _____

   _____

5. Because the chickens were faster than the kids . . .

   _____

   _____

6. Bonnie Belle started galloping in wild circles around the yard when . . .

   _____

   _____

Predict the Effect

Read the sets of causes below. Write the effect you might expect from each.

• •

1. Mom needed fuel for the cooking stove.
   Dad needed wood for the fireplace.
   I had time to help.
   Effect: _____

2. Corn was growing knee high.
   Weeds were growing nicely too.
   Mom needed help with the crops.
   Effect: _____

3. Locusts swarmed over our fields like brown clouds.
   Nothing could convince them to leave.
   We set smoky fires to drive them off.
   Effect: _____

4. Crows love corn.
   The corn was ripening fast.
   Mom gave me some straw and some old clothes to build something.
   Effect: _____

5. The cabin was too dark for reading.
   I could not light a fire in the hearth in the hot weather.
   A lantern sat on the table.
   Effect: _____

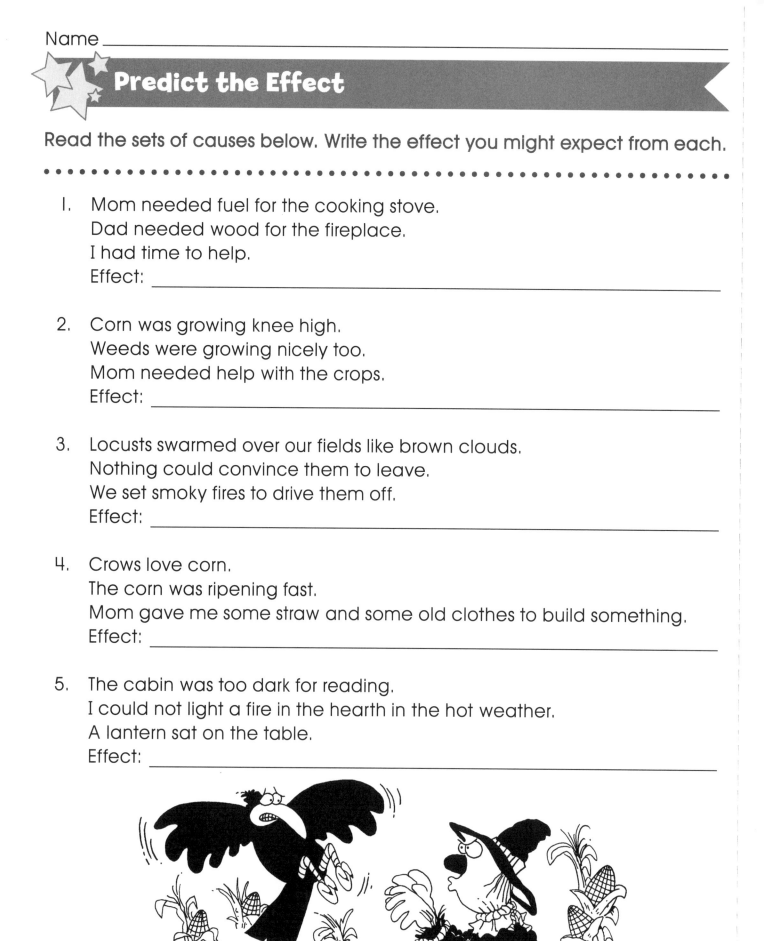

★ False Cause

Two events can occur near each other without one event causing the other. Read the following sentences. Decide if one event causes the other. Circle the correct answer.

• •

1. A black cat walked past Jake on the sidewalk just as a bucket of paint fell on Jake's head. The black cat caused the paint bucket to fall.

    A. true

    B. false

2. The man was painting the building's trim when a curious cat nudged his paint bucket from the roof. The cat caused the paint bucket to fall.

    A. true

    B. false

3. Each year, the Nile River floods the land and leaves behind moist, rich soil. Frogs, which are rarely seen when the ground is parched, are found in abundance in the mud. Mud creates frogs.

    A. true

    B. false

4. Every Sunday, Reba stays up late to watch her favorite television program. Every Monday morning, Reba has trouble waking up for school. Why does Reba have trouble waking up for school?

    A. because it is Monday

    B. because her favorite program made her late

    C. because she did not get enough sleep Sunday night

Name _____

When Hillary listens to the radio, it causes her to feel strong emotions. Predict the effect each segment has on her. Use the emotions in the word bank. Write your answers on the lines.

Emotional Effects		
angry	curious	elated
giggly	swooning	tired

1. Bob Bubble, host of "Hats Off to Laughter", shares a hysterical anecdote.
   Effect: _____

2. Roberta Snack, the newest star of the millennium, croons a song of romance.
   Effect: _____

3. News: All area schools will have three additional days in June due to education reform.
   Effect: _____

4. Sports Beat: The girls' high school basketball team has won the state championship.
   Effect: _____

5. Daphne Deltoid has completed her fifteen-minute "Aerobics on the Air" program. Hillary exercised along with her.
   Effect: _____

6. The station manager announces a new clue for the "Mystery Game" that Hillary wants to win.
   Effect: _____

On the Job

Ariel Speaks is press secretary to Mayor Bonnie Last of New Horizons, Connecticut. Read her schedule for April 14. Not everything goes as planned. Circle the correct answers to the questions below.

6:00 walk the dog	1:00 meet with Team 2
6:30 shower and breakfast	2:00 take care of correspondence
7:00 train commute to office	3:00 conference call with city council members re: recycling plans
8:30 arrive/check messages	
9:00 meet with Team 1	
10:00 tour recycling plant	4:00 formulate press release re: mayor's position on city-wide recycling
11:00 interview the plant's supervisor	
12:00 lunch meeting with Mayor Last	
12:45 call Kyle's teacher for a progress report	5:00 train commute home
	6:30 grab food from deli for supper

1. Because the plant supervisor called in sick, . . .
   A. Ariel could not meet with the mayor.
   B. Ariel was sent to Alberta.
   C. Ariel could not meet with him.

2. Because Kyle's teacher spoke for twenty minutes, . . .
   A. Ariel did not hear about her son's work.
   B. Ariel was late for a team meeting.
   C. Ariel missed lunch.

3. Because the train had a twenty-minute delay in the morning, . . .
   A. Ariel had no breakfast.
   B. Ariel could not check her messages.
   C. Ariel missed her meeting with Team 1.

4. Because Team 2 needed ninety minutes to go over problems, . . .
   A. Ariel had less time for correspondence.
   B. Ariel decided to call Kyle's school back.
   C. Ariel noticed cracks in the office walls.

Camp Letter

Read the letter Sasha sent to her friend from camp. Answer the questions on the next page.

• •

Dear Jen,

Camp so far has been great! I'm in a cabin with seven other girls and a camp counselor. Her name is Maya, and she's very cool. She lets us read after lights out, and she tells the best ghost stories ever.

Tasha is a really nice girl who is in my cabin. She's also on the Red Team with me. We were partners for the wall climb. That's one of our partnership challenges. We had to help each other climb up a bare wall with no steps or anything. It was hard work, but it was a lot of fun. We also had to build a cabin together using only natural materials. Our whole team had fun with that one. I'm hoping Tasha will be my partner for the trust fall we're doing tomorrow.

The food here is actually pretty good. Last night some of the counselors cooked dinner for us on the campfire. They made hot dogs and corn on the cob. It was great!

I miss all the kids back home on Russell Street, though. No one here wants to play cards with me. A lot of the girls only want to talk about what the boys are doing. And it is too bad that Mr. Torres cannot drive his ice-cream cart all the way out here to Gull Lake. I could really use a lime sherbet cone right now.

Well, I will see you at the end of the week. Give Squirts a hug for me.

Sasha

Name _____

1. Name two things that make Maya an "awesome" counselor.

   _____

   _____

2. Sasha likes being at camp because . . . (list three reasons)

   _____

   _____

   _____

3. Sasha misses home because . . . (list three reasons).

   _____

   _____

   _____

29

Long Ago

Connect each cause with its matching effect.

• •

Cause

_____ 1. The Princess kisses the frog.

_____ 2. There was a pea under the mattress.

_____ 3. Rapunzel was kept secluded in a high tower.

_____ 4. The Beast is kind to Beauty.

_____ 5. The fairy was not invited to Aurora's christening.

_____ 6. Jack cut down the beanstalk.

_____ 7. Cinderella's foot fit into the glass slipper easily.

_____ 8. Snow White ate the apple.

_____ 9. Grandmother was ill.

_____ 10. Humpty Dumpty had a great fall.

_____ 11. The youngster's porridge was gone.

_____ 12. The third pig built his house out of bricks.

Effect

A. He broke into so many pieces that all the king's men could not put him back together again.

B. The handsome prince married his lady.

C. She agrees to marry him.

D. The wolf could not blow the house down.

E. She fell into a deep sleep.

F. Baby Bear wailed.

G. She cast a spell on the child.

H. Red Riding Hood brought her cookies.

I. The giant fell to the ground.

J. The princess could not sleep.

K. He regains his human form.

L. She had never met any men before.

Name _____

Evan Denison is a busy sixth-grade kid. Look at his schedule. Circle the correct answers to the questions below.

Events

homework   football game

Schedule

6:00	alarm wakes up	12:00	shop for clothes
6:30	alarm wakes up again	2:30	chores
6:35	paper route	3:30	babysitting
7:30	breakfast	6:00	picnic supper
8:00	football game	8:00	watch wrestling on TV
10:30	new video game	9:00	homework
11:30	lunch	10:30	shower and sleep

1. Because his football game lasted three hours . . .
   A. he missed his paper route
   B. he couldn't play his video game for long
   C. he had fun
   D. he couldn't go shopping

2. Because his homework took longer than planned . . .
   A. he went to bed late
   B. he was tired
   C. he couldn't watch wrestling
   D. he went to bed early

3. Because his picnic dinner lasted until 8:30 . . .
   A. he did his homework late
   B. he skipped his paper route
   C. he missed part of his wrestling show
   D. he went to bed late

Name _____

★ Around the World

Below are facts about Ferdinand Magellan's famous explorations. Connect each cause with its matching effect. Write the letters of the correct effects on the lines.

Cause

_____ 1. Trading would make investors rich.

_____ 2. The Portuguese controlled the sea route to the East Indies.

_____ 3. Seamen prepared to ward off enemies.

_____ 4. The Spanish ships had a long journey across the Pacific.

_____ 5. The mapmakers had underestimated the size of the Pacific Ocean.

_____ 6. The shores the ships passed were illuminated by the fires of the American Indians.

_____ 7. The Portuguese controlled the African Cape of Good Hope.

Effect

A. Spanish explorers dared not travel south around Africa.

B. Ships were sent to the Far East to trade.

C. Magellan named this land Tierra del Fuego (land of fire).

D. The Spanish hoped to discover a different route to the Spice Islands by traveling west.

E. The trip took longer than expected.

F. They had to pack a lot of supplies.

G. The ships were armed with guns and cannons.

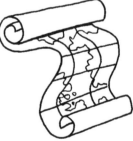

Can You Tell?

Read the sentence pairs below. Label the cause with a **C**. Label the effect with an **E**.

• •

_____ 1. Dogs bark at noises.

_____   Many people own them to protect their properties.

_____ 2. We call ants social insects.

_____   They live in colonies.

_____ 3. Newspapers can sell for reduced prices.

_____   Newspapers contain many advertisements.

_____ 4. Cats are extremely agile creatures.

_____   When dropped, cats land on their feet.

_____ 5. Few mammals can care for themselves at birth.

_____   Most baby mammals need their parents to take care of them.

_____ 6. The sun has a powerful gravitational force.

_____   The earth revolves around the sun.

_____ 7. Banana growing requires a tropical climate.

_____   Bananas are not grown in Maine.

_____ 8. People fear snakes.

_____   Snakes are described as evil creatures in many stories.

_____ 9. People must take precautions against skin cancer.

_____   The ozone layer is thinning.

_____ 10. Most television and radio commercials include music.

_____   Music helps recall our memories.

Whoops!

RUFF! RUFF! RUFF!

Domino Effect

Read the passage. Answer the questions on the next page.

• •

Have you ever set up dominoes so that if you knocked the first one down, it would hit a second one, which would hit the next one? Domino toppling is one of the simplest and most effective visible examples of cause and effect. Physicists use the reactions of simple dominoes to demonstrate abstract principles and complex processes in nature.

International Domino Art teams have a different goal when they topple the rectangular game pieces. They attempt to set world records. Television networks around the world have broadcast "Domino Day" to millions of viewers. The official record for the most dominoes toppled has been passing back and forth between Europe and Asia since 1986.

In December 2000, 62 Chinese, Japanese, and South Korean students got together in Beijing, China to break the European record. It took a month of meticulous effort to arrange almost 3.5 million colorful dominoes on the floor of an indoor recreation center.

On December 31, the first domino was tipped, setting off the anticipated chain reaction. As the other dominoes toppled, they formed pictures of animals, musical instruments, food, and famous people. There were even copies of paintings by van Gogh and Picasso. When it was over, more than 3,000,400 dominoes had fallen, and the world's record belonged to Asia.

In 2001, the Europeans created an even larger, more ingenious setup in Holland. It included a domino roller coaster and a Wild West display with "shooting" cowboys. They recaptured the record with 3,500,000 downed dominoes.

In the fall of 2002, 89 domino "builders" congregated in Leeuwarden, Holland to break the record again. They came from Germany, France, and Sweden. It took the international team eight weeks to set up 4,000,000 colorful dominoes in elaborate patterns and displays. On Domino Day, November 15, the first domino was knocked down.

The reaction lasted for over an hour and a half. When it was over, 3,847, 295 dominoes had fallen. Yet another record was set.

Domino Effect (cont.)

Read each pair of sentences. Label them as causes or effects.

. . . .

1. The official starter touched the first domino. _____

   He initiated a chain reaction that would continue for more than 90 minutes. _____

2. Most of the dominoes toppled. _____

   Each separate domino fell against its neighbor. _____

3. Occasionally one of the dominoes would resist tumbling. _____

   Movement in that part of the display would come to a halt. _____

4. Many of the workers who set dominoes are students. _____

   Students have the leisure time and physical endurance for the task.

   _____

5. Television stations are prepared to broadcast the event on a certain day.

   _____

   Domino setters must adhere to strict schedules. _____

6. The teams work hard for many months. _____

   The dominoes magically topple, creating fascinating designs and effects.

   _____

A Midsummer's Day Dream

Read the play's cast and synopsis below. Circle the correct answers to the cause and effect questions below.

. . . .

Cast

Argus—a young lord

Clarissa—a quick-minded female

Eureka—a scholarly maid

Fozzy—a scruffy joker

Benvolio—Argus's squire

Desdemona—Clarissa's maid

Synopsis: A young lord and his squire are returning home from the wars. They travel through a Greek village where they meet the beautiful Clarissa, a quick-minded woman with one goal: marriage. She and her maid, Desdemona, lay traps to win the hearts of the two men. Meanwhile, a scruffy joker courts the maid.

Act One: the forest

Act Two: the marketplace

Act Three: the churchyard

Act Four: the forest

1. Why are the two men walking through this town?
   A. They are returning from a war.
   B. They are lost.
   C. Their horses have run off.

2. The two soldiers should be on guard because . . .
   A. the Greeks are their enemies.
   B. a joker loves the maid.
   C. two ladies wish to capture their hearts.

3. The ladies are attracted to the men because . . .
   A. they want to get married.
   B. the men are handsome.
   C. the men are nicer than the joker.

> **Try this:** Create one of the following:
> • an opening line for Argus
> • a food-related four-line song for Fozzy
> • a short conversation between Clarissa and Desdemona

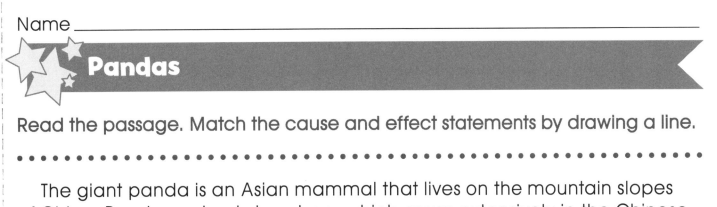

Pandas

Read the passage. Match the cause and effect statements by drawing a line.

The giant panda is an Asian mammal that lives on the mountain slopes of China. Pandas eat only bamboo, which grows extensively in the Chinese highlands. To get enough nutrients, a panda must eat as much as 85 pounds (39 kg) of bamboo a day. The rampant destruction of the panda's habitat has endangered this creature. The government of China has tried to save the panda's food supply by setting up reserves of bamboo-rich land. Large reserves are necessary to ensure adequate food for the pandas. Because bamboo plants take so long to grow into mature plants, there have been shortages in the past. However, the government continues to work to fix these shortages.

Cause

1. Pandas must get enough nutrients.
2. Bamboo takes a long time to mature.
3. There is rampant destruction of the panda habitat.
4. There have been bamboo shortages.

Effect

A. Pandas are endangered.
B. They must eat huge amounts of bamboo.
C. Periodic bamboo shortages occur.
D. China has set up bamboo reserves.

37

Ancient Farming

Read the passage. Answer the questions on the next page.

• •

The Inca, the Aztec, and the Maya were three ancient civilizations from the Americas. The Maya thrived in the area we know as the Yucatan and Central America. The Incan Empire was located along the west coast of South America in what are known today as Peru and Chile. The Aztec lived in the area we know as Mexico. Their capital city was in the same place as modern-day Mexico City. Agriculture was very important to all these civilizations.

For the Aztecs, the common agricultural tool was a pointed stick used for digging. In areas covered with dense forest, farmers practiced slash-and-burn agriculture, in which they burned a section of forest and planted in the cleared areas. In this way, the ashes from the burn produced highly fertile soil. In hilly or mountainous regions, the farmers cut terraces into the hills to increase the amount of flat farmland on which to plant. Farmers also built island-gardens, called chinampas. They scooped up mud from lake bottoms and made islands that were suitable for planting. The chinampas yielded huge crops.

The Inca used a variety of farming methods. Along the coastal desert, they built networks to help irrigate the land so plants would get enough water. In mountainous areas, they cut terraces into the hillsides as the Aztecs did. Their farm fields were divided into three groups. One field was dedicated to the needs of local people. The other two supported state and religious activities.

Mayan farmers built raised fields similar to the chinampas of the Aztecs. They used swampy lowlands and drained the soil to unearth fields on which to grow their crops. They combined this technique with terracing to provide food to feed large populations.

Ancient Farming (cont.)

1. Slash-and-burn agriculture produced highly fertile soil because . . .

_____

_____

_____

2. Aztec farmers built chanampas to . . .

_____

_____

_____

3. Many farmers built terraces to . . .

_____

_____

_____

4. Aztecs divided their fields into three sections because . . .

_____

_____

_____

Let's Get It Started

In a story or play, an event called the **inciting incident** forces a character to make a choice. The inciting incident is the cause. The choice is the effect. Read the inciting incident in the circle. On each of the empty lines, write an effect.

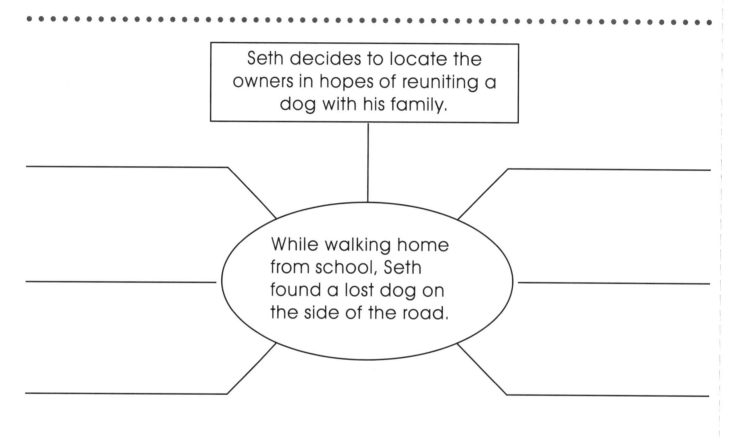

Seth decides to locate the owners in hopes of reuniting a dog with his family.

While walking home from school, Seth found a lost dog on the side of the road.

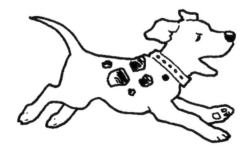

Name_____

The Dust Bowl

Read the passage. Answer the questions below.

A long time ago, many states in the mid-
and southwest were covered with thick grass.
Grass covered the land as far as the eye could
see. This land was called the grasslands.

Many settlers moved into the grasslands.
They used the grassy fields to graze livestock
like cows and sheep. Some settlers plowed
the fields and planted wheat. However, these
settlers used up the land so much, that it became barren.

Then, a six-year-long drought occurred. Little rain fell, and the sun
scorched the settlers' crops. Because there was no more grass, the soil
became loose. Strong winds caused the soil to form dust storms, covering
buildings and roads with dusty soil. Soon, even the air became clogged with
dust, and the people in these regions could not breathe. People began to
call this region the "Dust Bowl."

Things got so bad that many farmers were forced to move away. Farmers
in this region had to learn how to take care of the land. They planted trees
to break the strong winds off the grasslands. They also planted crops in strips
that followed the contours of the land. The strips created ridges that trapped
rainwater and allowed it to soak into the land. The farmers learned from their
mistakes and worked with the land to overcome the hardships of the Dust Bowl.

1. Farmland became barren because . . .

   _____

2. The land dried up because . . .

   _____

3. Farmers moved away from the Dust Bowl because . . .

   _____

4. Farmers planted trees to . . .

   _____

5. Planting crops in strips help the crops because . . .

   _____

Read the news articles below. Answer the questions on the next page.

• •

Terrible Storm Torments

A torrential storm hit Toon Town yesterday, causing a citywide power outage. When the strong winds sped through the town, light poles, bushes, and doghouses were blown down. Thankfully no one was hurt! However, much of the garbage spilled into the local lake. Officials urge townspeople to help in the clean-up.

Stores Closed All Over Toon Town

Business is not as usual this Monday in Toon Town. Stores all over are closed! McDuck's Department Store has a sign up front that reads, "Closed Due to Lake Cleaning." The owner, along with all of his workers, has been spotted picking up the trash that spilled in the storm. Business neighbors rush to join him. Houses in the main neighborhood also seem empty—there are no lights on! The lake area is swamped with people who are replanting bushes and sowing a new garden for flowers. The mayor gives big thanks to the people of Toon Town.

Town Picnic Postponed

As a result of yesterday's horrific storm, the Toon Town Picnic has been postponed. The mayor's office is reluctant to set a new date until the lake is cleaned up, although officials say it may not take too long with all of the help they are getting.

The picnic-planning meeting has also been cancelled until further notice. Committee members will be notified of its rescheduling. Anyone with concerns or inquiries should contact Daisy in the mayor's office.

Name _____

Write two cause and effect statements about each passage.

∙ ∙

1. Terrible Storm Torments

   _____

   _____

   _____

   _____

2. Stores Closed All Over Toon Town

   _____

   _____

   _____

   _____

3. Town Picnic Postponed

   _____

   _____

   _____

   _____

Try this: Write your own newspaper article.
Make sure you include plenty of causes and effects.

Name _____

Read the passage. Answer the questions on the next page.

• •

"What makes bread dough rise?" If you answered yeast, you are only partially correct. It takes more than yeast to turn flour and water into a sandwich-worthy loaf of bread.

Many things cause bread dough to rise. Wheat flour contains things called proteins. When wheat flour is mixed with a liquid, these proteins combine to form a material called gluten. As the dough is kneaded, gluten binds together to form a long sheet. If you stretch properly kneaded bread dough, it will form a membrane so thin you can see light through it. It is like looking through a translucent balloon. If you use flour that is not high in gluten-forming proteins, your bread will never develop those important gluten strands. If you do not knead the dough, the gluten strands will not form the long chains and sheets that help the dough rise.

Gluten alone does not make dough rise. We need to introduce yeast. Botanically, yeast is a living organism called a fungus. Baker's yeast feeds on material in the wheat and releases gas bubbles, just like the bubbles in soda. The gas becomes trapped in the sheets of gluten, causing the dough to expand like an inflated balloon.

It takes time for the yeast to produce the gas bubbles. Depending on the recipe and the temperature, bread may need only a couple of hours to rise, or it may need to rise overnight. If you mix and knead the dough to create gluten strands, but do not allow time for the yeast to work, you will bake a loaf of bread that looks and tastes like a brick. Your sandwich might send you to the dentist!

If you have done everything right to this point, you have almost accomplished your goal of a light loaf of bread. The final element is heat. Gases expand when heated. When your risen dough sits in the heat of the oven, the trapped gases expand, causing the dough to rise a little more. Bakers call this oven spring, or oven kick. Oven spring accounts for a small but delicious part of the overall rise. After a short time in the oven, the bread dough becomes firm and will no longer stretch. Your bread has risen as high as it will.

Now all you have to do is finish baking your bread. Allow it to cool, slice it, and make the best sandwich ever!

Science in Your Sandwich (cont.)

Match each effect to the correct cause.

- -

Causes	**Effects**

Causes

_____ 1. When wheat flour is mixed with a liquid . . .

_____ 2. Kneading bread dough . . .

_____ 3. Yeast . . .

_____ 4. Gas bubbles . . .

_____ 5. Time . . .

_____ 6. Heat from the oven . . .

Effects

A. produces gas bubbles that make the dough rise.

B. allows the yeast to work so that the dough rises completely.

C. protein mixes into gluten.

D. causes gases to expand until the dough finishes rising, so the dough can bake.

E. cause dough to rise, kind of like air inflating a balloon.

F. creates long sheets of gluten.

Answer Key

Page 4
Circle: 1. a; 2. c; 3. b; 4. a; 5. a

Page 5
1. C, E; 2. E, C; 3. C, E; 4. C, E; 5. E, C; 6. C, E; 7. C, E; 8. E, C

Page 6
Causes: 1. mowing lawns; 2. saved his earnings; 3. forgot to water plant; 4. Becca watered it. 5. studied very hard; 6. Carla made a perfect score on the test. Effects: 1. earned money; 2. could afford to buy a new bike; 3. plant wilted; 4. plant became healthy; 5. Carla finished the test easily; 6. brought her grade to an A

Page 7
1. b; 2. d; 3. a; 4. c

Pages 8–9
1. a, b, d; 2. c, e, f; 3. h, i, l; 4. g, j, k

Page 10
Answers vary. Examples:
1. You have a sore back. 2. You need a hot pack. 3. You need a cold pack. 4. break the water pouch; 5. mix the chemicals.

Page 11
1. He went to the beach. 2. He went shopping. 3. He saw a movie. 4. He was late to school. 5. He took too long in the bathroom. 6. He got an A+ on the assignment.

Pages 12–13
Calvin stayed in his house. g, j, i
We traded in our old car. b, d, e
The snake crawled into its hole. c, h, l
We played soccer. a, f, k

Page 14
1. Flowering plants are vital to bees. 2. Bees are diverse insects. 3. Bee colonies are complex. 4. Farmers depend on bees for livelihood.

Page 15
Underline: 1. Omar stubbed his toe; 2. The rain was coming into the house; 3. I was full from the tasty chicken soup; 4. she missed an easy lay-up; 5. we mixed vinegar and baking soda; 6. he was excited to fly for the first time; 7. the theater lights were turned on; 8. he is interested in modern art; 9. she had no kings; Circle: 1. he cried out, "Ouch!"; 2. we shut the window; 3. I slept like a baby; 4. Karen was disappointed; 5. It erupted; 6. David could not sit still; 7. I was blinded for a moment; 8. Ted begged to see the newest art exhibit; 9. Tanya said, "Go fish!"

Page 16
1. c; 2. d; 3. a; 4. b

Page 17
1. d; 2. a; 3. b; 4. c

Cause and Effect • CD-104552

Page 18
Underline: 1. President Jefferson was interested in finding a water route for trade to the Pacific Ocean; 2. her husband Toussaint Charbonneau was hired as a guide; 3. She was Shoshone; 4. he was only a baby; 5. To move the expedition's freight up river; 6. Because of her herbal knowledge; 7. when she met her older brother, now a chief among her people; 8. her husband was officially hired by the expedition and she was not; 9. There are conflicting reports about Sacagawea's later life; Circle: 1. he commissioned an expedition; 2. Sacagawea joined the Corps of Discovery; 3. Sacagawea could help Lewis and Clark's expeditionary force obtain food and supplies from her people; 4. Sacagawea carried her son on her back; 5. the group hired a large keelboat; 6. Sacagawea's tasks included gathering edible plants; 7. The young woman was surprised; 8. Sacagawea received no personal compensation; 9. historians consider her a puzzle.

Page 19
Circle: 1. The bus had a flat tire. 2. Josh needed help. 3. It had slipped under his dresser. 4. He hoped to find his grandfather's watch. 5. He had the address. 6. It was their first case in a long time. 7. They were late. 8. The house had a messy yard. 9. The dresser was in Josh's room.

Page 20
Answers vary. Examples:
1. She ate her food. She had yet to pack her lunch. 2. It was a school holiday. He already finished his homework. 3. He was catching the flu. He ate something unpleasant. 4. It was raining. The dog went swimming. 5. The oven was too hot. We left it in for too long. 6. It liked howling at the moon. It was scared of a man nearby.

Page 21
Answers vary. Examples:
1. He blew up the balloon. 2. She fell off her bike. 3. It was a snow day. 4. I won the race. 5. My mouth smelled clean. 6. Dani shared the burger with her dog.

Pages 22–23
Answers vary. Examples:
1. The chickens got loose. 2. told him Dad would be unhappy with him otherwise; 3. that is where all the noise came from; 4. The chickens had broken out of their coop. 5. The kids could not get them back in the coop. 6. She saw the chickens.

Page 24
Answers vary. Examples:
1. I helped chop the wood. 2. I helped weed and harvest. 3. The locusts went away. 4. I built a scarecrow. 5. I lit the lantern.

Page 25
Circle: 1. b; 2. a; 3. b; 4. c

Page 26
1. giggly; 2. swooning; 3. angry;
4. elated; 5. tired; 6. curious

Page 27
Circle: 1. c; 2. b; 3. b; 4. a

Pages 28–29
1. She tells the best ghost stories ever.
She lets us read after lights out.
2. Tasha is a really nice girl. The
whole team had fun. The food is
really good. 3. No one will play
cards. She could really use a lime
sherbet cone. Girls only want to talk
about what the boys are doing.

Page 30
1. k; 2. j; 3. l; 4. c; 5. g; 6. i; 7. b; 8. e;
9. h; 10. a; 11. f; 12. d

Page 31
Circle: 1. b; 2. a; 3. c

Page 32
1. b; 2. d; 3. g; 4. f; 5. e; 6. c; 7. a

Page 33
1. C, E; 2. E, C; 3. E, C; 4. C, E; 5. C, E;
6. C, E; 7. C, E; 8. E, C; 9. E, C; 10. E, C

Pages 34–35
1. cause, effect; 2. effect, cause;
3. cause, effect; 4. effect, cause;
5. cause, effect; 6. cause, effect

Page 36
Circle: 1. A; 2. C; 3. A

Page 37
1. B; 2. C; 3. A; 4. D

Pages 38–39
Answers vary. Examples:
1. The ashes make the soil fertile.
2. yield huge crops; 3. increase the
amount of land they had for farming;
4. They farmed for local people in
one area. The other two areas were
for state and religious purposes.

Page 40
Answers vary.

Page 41
Answers vary. Examples:
1. The farmers overused it. 2. There
was a drought. 3. They could not
breathe because of the dust.
4. break up the winds; 5. It helped
collect water.

Pages 42–43
Answers vary. Examples:
1. There was a power outage
because of the storm. Doghouses
were blown over because of strong
winds. 2. McDuck's Department
Store is closed because the workers
are cleaning the lake. Many other
stores are closed because everyone
is helping. 3. The picnic is postponed
because of the damage from the
storm. The mayor says the delay
won't be long because everyone is
helping out.

Pages 44–45
1. c; 2. f; 3. a; 4. e; 5. b; 6. d

Cause and Effect • CD-104552